Squandermania

Don Share

SALT

CAMBRIDGE

PUBLISHED BY SALT PUBLISHING
PO Box 937, Great Wilbraham, Cambridge PDO CB1 5JX United Kingdom

First published 2007

Printed and bound in the United Kingdom by Lightning Source

Typeset in Swift 9.5 / 13

ISBN 978 1 84471 294 6 paperback

Salt Publishing Ltd gratefully acknowledges
the financial assistance of Arts Council England

135798642

Squandermania

DON SHARE is Curator of Poetry at Harvard University, where he also teaches and serves as Poetry Editor of *Harvard Review*, and Editor-in-Chief of *Literary Imagination*, the journal of the Association of Literary Scholars and Critics. His other books include: *Union* (Zoo Press), finalist for the PEN New England/*Boston Globe* Winship Award for outstanding book; *Seneca in English* (Penguin Classics); *I Have Lots of Heart: Selected Poems of Miguel Hernández* (Bloodaxe Books), which received the *Times Literary Supplement*/Society of Authors Translation Prize; and a recently completed critical edition of Basil Bunting's poems. He is from Memphis, Tennessee.

Also by Don Share

I Have Lots of Heart: Selected Poems of Miguel Hernández
    translations, (Bloodaxe Books, 1997)
Seneca in English, (Penguin Classics, 1998)
Union, (Zoo Press, 2002)
The Poems of Basil Bunting: a Critical Edition,
    (Faber & Faber, 2008)

Contents

Acknowledgements

Portions of this book first appeared in *Artful Dodge, Cortland Review, Del Sol Review, Fulcrum, Pleiades, Ploughshares, Publio, Slate,* and *Yale Review*.

For Randy Chertow, with years of thanks.

I am grateful to those who encouraged this work: Forrest Gander, Jorie Graham, John Hennessy, Philip Nikoleyev, Tom Sleigh, and Rosanna Warren. And to my best and last reader, and best love, Jacquelyn Pope.

"the alphabet they could not squander"
— I.B. Singer (*The Last Demon*)

Once you say "A," you must say "B."
— I.B. Singer (*Yentl the Yeshiva Boy*)

Every soul descends to earth to correct some error. It's the same with souls as with manuscripts; there may be few or many errors. Everything that's wrong on this earth has to be corrected. This is the answer to all questions.
— I.B. Singer (*Three Tales*)

I.

Marooned

I'm an unreliable witness
I zone out

Hail, storm and tempest
you're marooned
in our marriage

again—

Have wizards knotted
snarls in our nerves,
nooses in our dreams?

Daughter born
in the land of granite
and cod's head,
we can't help where we live

A Nor'easter

again—

motes settle like sparks
from the attic's highest joist,
scar even the hidden niplet
of light heavened here

Don't ask for grace-notes
when the stave is starved

My beard is a grate
for the ashes that no mason frames,
but which fall so lightly, and land

marooned in the island,
alien, of our affections where

I saw nothing,
and heard the same

Meaning

It don't mean a thing
if it don't mean a thing

if I understand
your gist

Patience comes
to those who wait—

were we spiders
I'd be a bug-mummy by now

The wasp of Dedham
goes floating free—

sting me,
it don't mean a thing

Does science refute
my star-learning?

Do you?
A thing.

Which means
the stars are open

books.

The wedding
was a weeding

of two minds,
impedimenta such as

hollow tree trunks,
snow like rancid frosting—

I look
at my daughter

and the thing is,
I'm a dead man

Landmarks

"But a man, a fortiori myself, isn't exactly a landmark . . ."
— BECKETT, *Molloy*

Old streetsigns, posts
like tombstones

say: *Village, Church, School*

(On Court St. I am innocent
on Highland, I take the high road
on Ames I am aimless again)

They say: *Bridge, Summit*

Snow like plaque on the teeth
of our sore picket fence—

Who are these dumb dogs
visiting every small landmark?

The Library needs a new roof,
the Historical Society needs a new roof,
the Town Hall does,
the Court House does,
the Police Station does—

Who is ringing the doorbell *now?*
Is it the unrelenting oil of rain?
Winter's inability to listen to his wife?
Spring's promiscuous crocuses?
Fall's tired yellowing light and red leaf-parade?

Yes, yes, yes to all,
                    alike as eternity!

Ruby

In the belly of a swallow
there is a stone
which cures
      bad conceits, preserves

and insures
the good estate
      of the body.

I have never seen
an ebon stone
though my ancestors
      slaked their metal with it;

nor lodestone:
taken inward like viper wine
it restores youth, yet causes
      melancholy;

mercury, they wrote,
satisfies everyone;
sapphire is sky-colored;
      lapis purges.

I know that sea shells
are cordial, that coral drives
      away fear;

that gold, diamonds
are no better than poison,
      impostures always.

Of all the known magico-
magnetic cures
only garnet, my birthstone—
     kernel of pomegranate,

unperfect, a kind of ruby—
registers sorrow
then enchants the heart
     and expels fear

in this, our glitterbound microcosm.

Donny Doodle Furens

In a way, I feel
guilty that I did not die so
someone could inherit all this sooner.

I know you know, though,
that when I piss and moan, with
my head in my hands, I'm working.

When I'm happy, I'm not working.
I would be happier if . . .
the point of all this light

should be light, right?
The point of love should be
a single concealed point with impact

on the worlds above,
these ligatures and notations
(so peripheral to the ambiguous)

should prove that psycho-
pathology is a useless luxury
in a sick world.

Isn't immortality
a kind of insomnia?
A disruption of the body plan?

Magic xylophones
those nights when my shoulder
held your sleepy head,

you never had to dream
alone, despite the vain hope
of touching my own heart

with the alphabet,
which is all cross-row,
less than the least

of mercies,
that at best, let us stitch
together parentage and parts.

The rejected stone
is not a cornerstone,
posted alone

like a charm, inset
like the sounds caterpillars
make to get ants to care for them.

Like the spell under
which scorpions will waltz
in the sexual pinch, claw to claw:

nature's perfect senses,
ours shallow and slow
to die, above all

you wish I wasn't living
with you anymore,
your sprung rhythm

now cannot be, counter-
pointed, rendering
me pointless after all.

So much for seeming
in equality, and all
those other stresses.

Once again, I find
angels afloat in Hopkins'
boat-like stanzas, all wrack

and wreckage and faith
in the bookless desert laid
upon memory and in memoriam.

Where do I land?
What is this place?
Our long journey from bliss

to bliss took us
where passion drove us
crazy, where the tongue,

gong-like, fears and fails
to go, where thoughts
are floss and land
bound up in thin trust

or covenant, where
everyone is an infant
again, with grasping growing

hand, with lasting glowing
tears on puffed cheeks
and where we walk clumsily

from rock to rock
with no flights of innocence
or verse winged from dust

and dream of house and root
and family tree, tooth
and nail proverbial, or cliché—

have it your way!

the very vein
of personality, pre-grief
with no relief, suspense not exactly

killing me, but data,
which almost rhymes with paranoia,
as I tell my kin and kith:

"If these are the woods,
I'm not out of them yet,"
the trail of the human

serpent over everything,
so much to repent,
the way, born with perfect

pitch, we end, in effect,
up with relative pitch
instead, to tell

that the voice of a woman
and the voice of a man
differ yet speak the same

words, divided
only in the incidentals:
a wailing wall in every garden—

my arteries, yes, harden
in the halls, so dark,
of insomnia

which, I infer,
rhymes with paranoia—
here comes the crush again,

where are the lost tribes
now that we need them?

the memories that come
easily, but wrong?

The Mystery Letter

What is the mystery letter
in the word, cry?
Why is monosyllable
not one?
At what age does one fail
to thrive?
When does the paring knife
lose its edge?
—How can you tell?
The last passenger pigeon flew
where, and left its brother doves . . . why?
What is the spirit of the letter,
the letter of the law?
The mystery letter is . . . why
the mystery?

The Seventy Interpreters

Conning
the lexicon
I feel
conned—

Who
boiled
and canned
our argot
again?

Sugar came
from cane, but
corn syrup,
fructose:
choices?

Where the sweet-
ness
of our fruitful
tongue buds?

No more
now for
fortune,
just torture
hath consumed

all
her arrows
upon us

∿

Our
one
mourning
dove,
though,
calls.

≈

Magico-
magnetic cures,
incubus and
inconvenience?
No,
not at all,
not
this time.

Ptolemy's
seventy
interpreters
couldn't change
the world:

white grass
grows
outside
the house
while the horse
starves.

≈

Where
are
my co-
relatives?

Oh,
petty
movables!

Everything
we own
has
two handles:
one
to be
held by,
the other not.

For this
we live.

Food for Thought

Never weaned from anger
(the stars incline but do not require),
left alone she thinks hard

thoughts mean as snow
at harvest: home is paradise
to cats, hell for wives, she thinks,

are all babies slippery?
boys hate old men, but women
despise them: she thinks,

bed full of bones,

and bad usage
aggravates the matter

She had a smack of this disease—
like Vulcan he made creaking
shoes for his Venus,

that is to say, being blood-
thirsty, Nature turns leaves
red every single fall, and she thinks

love more violent

Even Noah, Jerome says,
"showed his nakedness in his
drunkenness

which for six hundred years
he had covered in his soberness."

So what can she do with his
scores of years for scruples?

The sailor doesn't see the water
passing underneath his ship;

the fisherman all the fish deep
in the sea around his nets —

So, she thinks, nothing
will ever be my own, not even time,
and feeds herself more thoughts

the way ravens fed Elijah:
invisible, invisible, invisible

I morti

Do repeated messages have a cumulative weight?
If so, my unvirtuosic disposition
will have lost patience, will lose
the questions themselves —
like carpets, unrolled,
of sod in sodden springtime.
A false new seediness takes root,
damaging persons, marooning me here with supple
rage, which claims a green plot, nourishes
dubious hopes of a different genetic unfolding.
Neatness, nature hastens to remind us,
is all. Even the trees, replete
with arcing inchworms working earthward,
bow, as we know, their spot-eyed heads waving
through the winds of vivid storms;
they can be bereft only of so much.
I open the window. I polish my glasses.
I let imperfect perceptions
take the meanings they appear
destined to take, given synapses, the earth's reeling
spectacle, its atmosphere of blind need,
this ultimate vacuum,
the naked sense of having been blessed.
Cat, sunspot, aurora, rose?

II.

Rest

Sabbath is a river that flows
every day but Sunday,
yet there is no rest
from war.

The velocity
of its ferocious light
is its maximum possible velocity,
even in the spired
faculty of the soul
with all her longing and avidity.

Bitter in the belly
but honey in the mouth—
copious resin of experience—
are these *cryptonyms, influentials.*

Firmly rooted as dogwoods, as axioms,
each star casts about again
for more of its core to burn

while below,
our sole garden is italicized
by crime, the first and last of things:

Justice is conflict,
not the other way around.

The Counterfeiters

With what analogical objects can one tell
when a war begins? If forced, as a mother,
to choose between man and baby, well,
of course you choose the baby;
and so goes casualty and causality: and sin.
For this we do not blame or displace or dispel
mothers in our blood, or in its heart-rended terminus,
or even in this my ode on the counterfeiters. No,
September was a warming, so some took wedded . . .
I was going to say bliss . . . this will have to be
pastiche, or burlesque, at best; but you know,
we'd assumed that everything would be all right.
Then came collision, and the wary tides
of fear, all the codes and chains of life blown
out of currency. The Eastern brother and the Western
brother met as if they'd never fully known each other.
Each wished the other dead, it turned out. Strangely,
fertility brushed and flossed, read a story, and went to bed.
So who dreamed that this war would begin?
Who dreamed this first red apple of the fight?
The dreaded blue screen of death?

"This building is alarmed" (anger language)

strange fruitions
when it's dark you light a candle

"like crow, like egg
cut to her kind ..."

if the dam trot
the foal will not amble

she may relent
but she may revert

The pyracantha thorns scrape the side of our house
saying, "War ... war ... war ..."

As we wind and unwind our devotions

At Home

Greetings to the red-eyed clouds
from this, the house that sits

on the mound and faces the corner
that marriage built, where wine

was drunk and semen flooded
the egg which lodged in the uterus

that built the daughter who greeted
the man and the woman here

in the mound at the corner in the house
that education built, and you

know from home-schooling
that the woman can be the teacher

and the man can be the tender child
and ditto the actual infant, depending

on her sex, dependent on love and
income; oh our dear dependent

is ruining the new chair in the house
that nested ambition built, along

with naked sense, and the beak
of god, the job of love, the hurt

of older homes, the hang
of it generally, the hands of pain,

the haze of Zoloft and the pudge
of Prozac, the twins of failed

marriages that manage to live on
in the ardor of our redone arbor

here in the house that books built,
that Yiddish and the Common Book

of Prayer built, that Presbyterian pride
built, that pogroms built, that blue

and white collars built, that Bildungs-
romans built, that the Biltmore built,

that mad dogs bayed at, that the baby
was born in that the cat bit and mouse

whispered within, over which, mortgaged,
the thunder caught its tongue and brought

great downpours upon while the coffee boiled,
while the paper, delivered late again, said:

We fight the terrorists abroad
so we don't have to fight them at home.

Medea in Reverse

I.

Little did I know
that during the wedding reception
my soon to be late-father-in-law secretly doled out
knives to his daughters,
which they were to conceal
in their gowns till, at his signal,
each would pierce
her husband through the heart.

Who would chance
his life by marrying a murderess?
On the other
hand, what wedding night passes
without disaster?

A Terpsichore
began the dance.

II.

After all, Paradise can't exist
till it's gone; the rest

of life, lived
in the half-light of anxiety,
is endless, as we know it,
the very opposite of genealogy:

So
my father-in-law
was, as a terrible husband and father,

condemned to the end-
less task of carrying pain
in his heart,
that clay jar perforated like a sieve.

After his own sandstorm marriage,
and a hail of children,
they say that a desert of thirst
forced him to capitulate, and recapitulate.

III.

Just as the Romans,
who did not have weeks,
were not exactly poor,
we squandered everything on love-
letters, those leaves in search of a forest.
In due course, juxtaposed,
we coalesced in marriage
at the church by the river
among vernal vivid tulips, happy
as if no season could be altered by grief.
Our household, unlike grief, ended.
All its intolerable moments,
like crevices weeping in winter,
were teethed with ice most inhuman.
Spiders wrapped their bug-mummies,
we un-bowed gifts,
while the spade-hands of our wedding clock
leaped from tick to tock. *Fix things up,*
her father advised,
before the snow.

His daughters spared the men,
as they were prone to do, at the last minute.

IV.

The scholar has his books.
The cardinal his villa, the skeleton of a cat he adored.
Your all-knowing father had his velleity,
yet he was absent, or absent-minded.
As for us:
You had your furrowed reflections,
the way a mariner has whalepaths.
I had impossible night thoughts,
tremulous visions in bat-light,
innominate phantasmata with their own wild justice.
Ours were the duels of archangels,
cardsharps, theologians, critics.
We fought, murmured, gave up ghosts,
and slandered each other,
as ever,
affluent, bull-headed, misprisoned to the very end.

Translated from the Potato Yiddish

Take heed of your wife's
    speeches in the pm
        and curtain sermons in the am

Whatever she engeminates,
    you value, too,
        and when you feel sad remember

One thing we had:
    the last night of the Philistines—
        never mind Raphael's baby Jesuses!

Being Jewish is owning
    the dark shadow that trails you
        and wrestling with seeds

And with the Sower—
    some were choked, some fell on barren ground
        and some cried quittance.

Ovum

(One of these poor "time-thieves"
    at the superstore—)

(I always thought I'd have a painter
    friend who'd paint me)

    (A changeling)

(The unnameable person
    and the unspeakable act)

(Post-partum, pre-menopausal)

    (The owls of indignation)

(The moon a blank void ovum)

Father Cannot Yell

after the song by Can

A sad-lidded blonde my age
follows a fat truffle of a man my
age wearing a shrunk I BEAT

ANOREXIA t-shirt
all belly and breath—
he hasn't been born yet!

she wears a string of stones
that follow the moon in silence,
that should keep love between man

and woman (unlike diamonds),
keep man from dreaming
in his sleep, protect him

from falling into a hole
and breaking all his bones
(is he losing his grip

or is it just weakening?)
she was head over heels,
more heels than head, with him

when she tried to scratch out
her life like a bad draft:
his Army buddy, a fatalist

with good reason
says, *it was her party,*
she could cry if she wanted to,

suggests he quit his job
leave her and the kid behind, go
to the Holy Land, even, but

he hasn't been born yet!
a new life—to hunger, grieve, to
be what he is instead of what

he's become, but now even
the Dead Sea is dying—
it hasn't been born!

This man, this woman: their family tree
still holds some promise for new life
though man waits in ambush for man,

votive candles catch fire
and are recalled, and slumped in a pew
she thinks, *My desires are muddled*—

then the sermon comes on,
"the soul of the sluggard desires
and has nothing," because

he hasn't been born yet,
he hasn't been born! she dreams
about maps of tenderness while

glass-eyed as a needle
in the dark he can't make out
the distinct or the indistinct,

he's given each creed the benefit
of the doubt though now
it's more doubt than benefit,

and the sermon says, "some vines
have the propensity to grow
to the right, some to the left" —

so what fact under the sun is
invariable? *he hasn't
been born yet*, it's summer,

starting just as the peepers go
quiet, as woodrot chews the fence,
as wintermoth worms inch down

from branches invisibly
drawn to her hair as she gardens,
as roses nod over the rails

like clothes hung to dry:
a petal flashes in sun, a lost
silver leaf

of the Domesday Book?
if the coming thunderstorm
kicks up a strong head of wind

is God then copying
out all their accounts
on that one lost leaf?

no proofs of regime change or
Kingdom Come—Father cannot yell,
and someone is crying

he hasn't been born yet, he hasn't been born!

III.

Failure to Thrive

Your pregnancy, my nausea;
Rain again, the moths
      of motherhood; and

Zen marriage: *please don't*
Put that coffee cup on my
      kitchen table!

Glacial irreality of the some-
Things-never-changing. Where is love
      relucent?

Useless gifts, the ovum,
Reluctant grace.
      How do you feel?

These are "issues" —
There's a slight uptick in
      the grade of the road

Leading toward our house
I don't think you've noticed yet.
      Wheels spin

Through it so fast they start
To move backwards.
      We are meat

That sees, and when we die
Nobody eats us. Black umbrellas
      meet in the rain,

The end of the day is about
To become the beginning of a day.
    A script of weeds,

Post-partum, is learning its lines
For the very first run of love
      in this our microcosm.

Digression of Air

Thinking in semi-diameters
I etch my place on stone,
lichen-like, because I don't lie
enough, itself a form
of lying.

The freshening of Atlantic waters
is a sign of cold currents to come,
climate-change,
the wrath and roll
of earth.

Venus in transit
through the moved sky
which is not sky moving there,
but a quilt, just enough,
of pining.

Laughing at isobars and thorns
pinioned on the naked
weather map you wonder
when will we ever learn
enough

of lying, earth, pining: *enough*

Fiery Crash or Ferry Crash?

The sun warms Ground Zero
        as if it had nothing else to do:
a cursing and a bless.

There are lots of bobbing news-
        papers trailing off
in the headwind; and

I think we set the clocks back
        on Sunday.
Now the birds veer.

How do they know how many
        birds aflight make
the optimal vee? When

is their flying ended, when,
        when their flying's ended,
do they fly apart singly?

What is in the mind of these
        vees? Wings
and burning sheets are shuttling

us between seasons . . . we never stop
        thinking and we never shut up:
disaster marries us, in this our microcosm.

Explicit

The lights went out: I thought,
Here's where the past ends ...
I spoke too soon! Or not ...

No, *here's* where the past ends ...
Each moment seized, lived, done-for,
Future an open-book or door no more.

The moon mends, heaven portends,
So here's where the past *ends*,
Here, here, dear friends ...

Today's gone tomorrow; so beg, borrow
Or steal time from the marrow
Since there's where the past ends ...

Loose ends, godsends, bygones
Gone by, gone in two-by-twos,
Who *knows* where the past ends,

O rock, redeemer, rock of ages
Pressed between salvages of dry pages
Saying here's where the past ends ...

Then send in the clowns, and *soon*,
And do not send to know for whom
Nowhere is where the past ends ...

The Sandpaper Ministry

No imprimatur, yet, not
of mother or father:

Nor of ghosts, angry
and obsessed.

Like the blackbird's catches
these are unapplied energy.

Not a stroke of genius,
but a stroke nonetheless:

Lightning portamento
conceived in June or April.

"... *not that we did evolve
from birds; we were only reptiles
together* ..."

"... *emotion devoid of earth* ..."

The gasp line
in a wild goose chase ...

Let me hammer in
these old nails I left loose.

I see the intelligent design
of your shriek marks,

arched eyebrows,
terse,

"staggered tandem over time . . ."
you are no globalist,
pregnant.

Our house is not a
homonym, yet.

Here we worried
about ticks, rabbit fever,
in which the sins

of the mothers multiply,
are visited willy-nilly

upon the sins of the sons
and vice versa,
and so on.

And now this reversible
versicle:
a song cycle.

Labor is fickle commotion,
a wombling an unlost
labor of love

in which exhausted mama
counts mammalian
contractual obligations.

In matrimonial ligations,
word is not quite
bond,

but birthing can by no man
be undone, never,
even if the father doesn't bother.

So, dear daughter,
(whom we got and begot, besotted!)
we shall never forget or regret

your foray: into the world
you come,
          welcome!

and come, o ligatures and accents grave.
Not for her, new loss-causation,
the defendant's secret weapon . . .

          Every step
she takes toward life
is a blade chased

on the whetstone,
cord-blood sere
on the serrated edges

of time's starving teeth,
biting daily, the deadly
gradations yet living

to make fit the taste, the corpus.

Healing slowly as sumacs
blossom burn-brown in growing heat,
boasting autumn's color before the fact.

The fact: the anniversary rosebush
died in a week, a week.
Its heart was put out.

I was shaken.

Now, in the sandpaper ministry
of the second-best bed,

our days are full, and sleep
comes hard. No time . . .

Shall we ask half mercy?
They do not grant halves in heaven.

Only on earth are we dividual:
only when we quarrel we are individual.

Meantime hair grows out gray,
teeth yellow and fail while violence lacks

no imagination, heartlessness
no limit—

The fallacy of misplaced
concreteness strikes again

and again, in spite of which
berries redden on the pyracantha—
O our autumnal love and child.

Born to her great state, and estate:
this house was built to live in,

no want of fruitfulness here
or ill air abides, just fair room.

The lowest trees have tops,
says Dyer, long dead now.

Nerves die in age, and all
that remains is the ipso facto tangle—

I can't even think "soul" anymore,
Maddy, I leave you,

you inherit me.

Buddy Holly *Gold*

The mother tongue
is subtle, cool,

monographic—

only Dante weighed
the boat down

on the Styx, so
why do I stare

at his heavy book
as if I were

looking in the mirror?

Joke shops are always
in bad neighborhoods,

hemmed in,
hawed in—

false glasses,
mustaches—

you laugh, but when
fortitude turns

to madness, father-
less, botherless, it's

like forcing flowers
to reach through air

to find peace there for hours
in the roots' fingerlings —

Isn't heaven then
the absence of sea and earth,

a place without walls?

who knows the spinkings
of our maker —

humid, gyroscopic, mosaic —

as we, set free, set sail,
dissolve toward those

destinations without
terminus, God bless us,

everyone turned
by love to the natural,

leaning to wonder;
so as to ask

those we left behind —
extroverted materialists to a man

who leaf through
the codex for direction —

What's the matter,
dolorosa?

Why are you gazing
against the grain?

You can't see stars
in hell, or in a city,

yet D. mourning V.,
B. calling D. in

the icefields of sin,
where one good turn

deserves no other
(take your time, turn in),

the old fools ask again,
Where are the stars

I've never seen before?
Here's dawn, and a dim

one, at that, where we commence
to feed the greed

pump back behind
the dun red door

of rain in West
Tennessee,

farming fear in the seed-
land and stock market,

cursing the black pooled
waters of hazard

inland from the Gulf,
oil subdicted

at the wishing well
of money, sight

unseen, in gold array,
near-pandemic diamond brightness,

tribal cash and trees
burning for days

in the mean glitter, spool
and pollen of a dark

burning round clouds
at the glacial sky-edge

where fingernail
moons and lost space-suits

radio back their half-
answers (take your time

and mine, too),
their chess games and Meccas

trembling amid the spoil
of bad texts and worse caricatures

scattered like whispers
in the forbidden wind-shakings—

The woodpecker is
at the wall again,

somebody please feed
the hummingbird

with unfathomed
tremolos, oddly edifying

and afloat like ivy
and words or mosses

o warming globe,
o good memory and tinnitus—

we draw together among scratchy
Bo Diddley maracas and artsy

Lennon/McCartneys,
always a bridesmaid,

always a bride,
equally painful in

the static of a fool's
paradise—

Why call them *oldies*

where Peggy Sue
got married

and I got lost with you
in the opaque hushings

of these old quarries?

"An old image in arras hangings"

Love you dearly like pig and pie:
Living with you in ingress, egress, regress—

marriage unfinished, fresh as a fire
and how the preparatory joys of paraphrase

are fleecy seeds in the sun.
Yet we are differenced, naked

like tears that start in the eyes
and descend to the neck: We see

and are undone because each eye
is a secret orator who knows

that $2 + 2 = 4$
but also that 2×2 also $= 4$

Ah, si liceret! That I might!
And act on temptation

without beginning to die on that day
in fraught monosyllables, O to

reach the goal of copia
in just so many words.

Donkey was created so men would not
have to say *ass; rooster* not *cock*—

but then the old masters also avoided
marjoram! Is it too much to ask

for balsam kisses, a salad of tongues,
for herbs and oil to garnish our super-

substantial daily bread? The stars
are above me, but what law

is within me? As the ancient Greeks
called the sea barren or unfruitful

homesick as they were for their vines,
I find the seasons with you seasonable, spiced,

mock-heroic. Even my faith is more faithful,
my lovetalk laureled, my books books.

Yet you remember memory instead of me.
Once we were innocent not just *nocent*

and in a sense the veil of evil has been drawn tight.
We withdraw into mood as the world wars on . . .

This is love. Nights upon nights we dream distinctly,
which is what makes fate so fatal. You won't cradle

my head in your lap, OK, so eternity will.
A child can laugh and cry at the same time

and forget everything and remember, too—
As the "glue or lime with which the wings

of the mind once taken cannot fly away,"
I will always ask childish things: Where

is the dust of a dove's heart, a stone
from the eagle's nest, and what, exactly,

is the doctrine of our pulses? Insomnia's
sting has left a crust in the corner of my eyes,

the sediment of my blood longing
like its distant kin the bleached sand in

Maddy's sandbox. And now she issues
invitations scrawled on sandpaper

in contusion and rasp, her hurt nails
white and rubbed down to red.

These sheets on sheets, blankets of dreams:
How to grasp our story together?

The wallpaper sheds its hokey old
Victorian patterns in sheaves of paper leaves,

down curls the dun-colored paint that darkened
every long shadow we shared. We spend

fronds of cash that bend low in this harsh
September storm, and the radiator's iron

will kicks in. A still snake warms itself
on the page, exhales simmering letters

like the simmer and steam of our great iron pot.
The sippy cups of spring have given way

to summer's cluster-rains and raw sun.
Now autumn's winter grandly occupies

the dull haze of our pewter, everything
antique, inherited, except this war and our fear

which goes by bleeding and fighting.
There are too many souls for God to bless,

unless that's Him doing the Limbo over
us all; and in the end these documents,

my prayers, are clear as water yet
illiterate and hopeless like the threads

of their gestation. I forget
who it was who was praying

for the common yellow lily or blue jay
in our yard, whose these prayers flowing

more prayers: What river do you imagine
wouldn't return to the sea in the end?

Maddy's New Rhyme

Clock. And *dark.*
Millennia of dark ink, not blood,
illuminate the paper-thin walls
of our kindred veins: it's the dead
who keep us going,
because they couldn't live without us.
It's because of them that we
have to keep going.
So the sprawlings of hair on the sink—
brown, hers; black, mine—
curl into question marks.
What if the terrorists strike again?
What if I don't live to see my daughter thrive,
or she survive to escort me to my grave?
Larger questions:
Who will be free? Who will die?
What is paradise?
Too hard. As it is, Maddy
looks out the window and asks, why
are there wounds in the ground
here ... here ... here ... here?
Eyes wide as watercolor daubs,
she is my microcosm. Maddy and Daddy
eat lunch in the kitchen, and she asks
whether seeds are lonely;
no, I say to myself, not so long
as the rabbits and robins
outsmart the elastic snow.

I Will Go Out For More

You held up bread, to make peace between us.
I held out my fist, with all the cleverness
of a backloader on dry land, plow an open claw.

In my roaring I am a father, and no father at all: your father.

I have made you something now you weren't destined to be.
My heart is split like the soft spiky scalp
round a fallen chestnut.

You, my seedling, my days, my law.

All promise lies with you, as in the grain we raise.
At the end of each harvest, I laugh or cry.
This time, you know the ending.

Earth cracked so that the seed of wheat could enter into it.
The rain cries, and farmer-fathers cry out
to farmer-mothers in their share of work and pain.

This bread you hold out—
We must all subsist on it; and when it is gone

I will go out for more, I will go out.

Lustre

Cut like a diamond, stars, frost, the corona of the sun,
Remote, keen, uncommon, bright. A shining body, or form.
Splendid beauty, more glorious than profitable. Never
diminished or out of fashion. Unfurling in an intimate arc
over China cups, your fingers, the stirring spoon stirring tea.
It was lustres ago, this. Skin like taffeta, hair from the handloom,
eyes lit like lanterns: like unlikeness. It's gone,
your talk, your silk, the ilk and milk of your cheek
and walk. You grasped your thoughts so firmly.
Every sentence was A, B, C, strung by joining-hand
in memory,—but you were elsewhere, and are now, and now.

Bottle in the Smoke

Pulling up ivy vines is like
grasping at any mystery: nothing
unravels, everything is tethered
to nothing, all is interdicted . . .
Black flies bite because I sweat,
as my ex-wife would say in her mordant
wit: because I am sweet. My hair
dangles, rooted, like ivy, in—
everything, in tangles of shallow
earth, and I grimace like a bottle
in the smoke here where long-
term memory criss-crosses short:
tenacious age soots up my fifth
decade, and no gracious revelations
will be reeled off now. Roots
sink slow, but blossoms arise avidly
—why do I still miss her?—
in this our microcosm.

Sweet Water, Best Bread

Bread, kneaded with rainwater,
failing that, with pure light thin
fountain water that arises in the east
and flows forever eastward, failing
that, water from a quick-running spring
from flinty, chalky, gravelly ground,
failing that, water from the longest river
you can find, failing that, muddy, still,
thick water left to settle for a day or two,
or even well-water lifted in dark old stone
cisterns—and if nature won't afford you
these your purest water must then be had
by art at infinite cost, and in rudiments.

Men Pretending to Sleep

Through babies' crying and churchbells.
Through edgy bad dreams on stifling nights.
Through fierce morning nuzzlings as the furnace fires.
Through mice scraping in walls, through too-close
for-comfort thunderclaps. Around the first
of the Fall, we let the lawn grow longer and drink
up sunlight. Winds come, then rains, not ferocious.
Finally the sere leaves begin to
drop: dream
quickens as we just-so-slowly stir. Curtains
wrinkle and grapple in an infant breeze.
Is this when our hair goes gray, when our house
sinks, sills and all, without so much as a moan?
Home ... everything shifts here, and I am,
or am I, sleeping, or pretending to sleep,
through it all. I was born like her, and like her
will die a man alone for real. Silent stars or war,
babies, bells, mice, thunder, don't wake me—don't.

IV.

To Father

To father is a verb
He said pauseably, absurdly,
Which swived me,

Such a thought
Is never (mercifully) finished,

Since fatherhood is mixed
With the Fall and all . . .

So the common Eve
Sews up the commonweal
Of mother wool

So wits wear down
In skeins as fingers

Fuss a-tremble
With the thimble: they falter.

As a rose's milk or sugar
Succors us in dwindling mothlight,

O, Father you can no
Longer keep me in the custom

To which you were styled,
Turning at every breath

My halting adumbrations,
My heritage, wild viper vine —

The baby's long cry and reach.

Intelligent Design

Cats love the devil, dogs are melancholy
(they never forget a farce), while as a lover,
Calypso'd, I was born for trouble among dream-
ladies talking lots of *ardzi, bourdzi,* and *loulas.*
Losing games of canasta and bets on the weather,
they can't believe in He "Who created fish, so ugly, bugs . . .
ach!" — the skin of progerics and other neologisms
of disease, disaster, and near-miss. Him
as conchologist, ignoring the fire in the garden;
we, living through revenge-effects, e.g.,
anti-depressants make certain people violently depressed;
testing a safer system causes reactors to explode;
more freeways create more traffic;
the power grid dims, powerless;
antibiotics make stronger germs. Swell.
Everything seems to be in apple-pie order, so
wine at night, coffee at dawn, till I reverse the routine,
I listen, not with a poker face (no gambler I), but
a solitaire to headline news from the Grand Guignol.
The cats and dogs are abandoned to rain,
asleep while storms are born with names
which gradually engrave stones as Gorgon,
egged on and *ex cathedra* to boot,
rears again her half-human unregenerate head.

Squandermania, or: Falling Asleep Over Delmore Schwartz

The moral superiority of distress
was limited, in my family, by *Kinderfeindlichkeit*.
As alternative commodities, we were lacking
        in economic utility, hence
        The Rotten Child Theorem,
the fostering not of children, but debt and guilt,
in exchange for which we admit our own deficiencies.
        I had two friends named Aaron.
        Both stuttered; neither was happy.
Their brother, Moses, was oddly favored by God.
The rod raised, no child in their pod was spoiled,
        and still, post-partum,
        the Red Sea parted with a great *Oy!*

One of the Aarons had a dog, a cat, a goldfish,
and imaginary friend, all unnamed. The other wished
        he was a woman named Elaine.
        Both played in the rain, alone,
shunned — stoned — by other boys and their brothers. Sad.
        How sharp it is, like a serpent's tooth,
        Their mother misquoted, *to have*
a thankless child! The Aarons dutifully read
Lear and *Hamlet*, hated their fathers and women,
        and kicked me hard.
        I was no paste-eater, but it stuck
with me that the ciphers we each learned, by rote,
made me a cipher. *Underfoot,*
        my mom called me,
        a cousin, I thought, to *Hiawatha.*

Presidents were father figures in those days;
we were taught that they were good, especially
        the ones from Ohio.

You don't want to hear about this,
It's worse than playing Monopoly. Or solitaire.
I digress. Where was Father? Working.
        I picture him now, jerking
        off his belt to mete out pain in penta-
metric slashes, punishment, in meaty welts I felt
        for ages. Only men who landed
        on the moon were proficient enough
for him, and nobody goes there anymore.
        Plenty of zero-G at home.
        Homo economicus, I call him now;
his job was to make everything small.
A small fish in a shrinking pond, he put the fun
in funereal, while Mom, rebarbative herself,
        shushed me irrepressibly
        and cued the frictive assault: a spanking!
Pardon the shriek-marks! What everyone
seems to know is how to fatten with rue,
        to live in controlled breakdown.

Yet to paraphrase The Who: *Who Are You?*
I've come a long way from *tohu wabohu*
—no? To be lectured? Am I in need of further
        admonition and correction?
        As opposed to instruction?
Then you, and you, and anyone who was here before
my zygote mitoseed into personality and gumption,
        What once was called, admiringly,
        grit, before the word meant a mote
in the eye, to be plucked, I shall defy, I say, I *defy*,
in *italics*, each reprimand, all getting-in of licks,
        and associated hissy-fits.

Try as you may, I am inured
to such reified . . . Reified what?

No word follows "reified."
    "Oh yeah? Sez who? You
    and what army?"
I was beaten again, the story
of my life, so again, I wake into, what else, my life?
    But I digress, in this mess. I,
unlike Lorca, am no good with the *Ay!*
am better with my eye, close-reading the stuff
of verse, perversely highlighting what's lost in translation.
    So don't cavil me with your
    critical cavalry: I write on, anyway,
by-and-by, and big boys don't cry. True,
my mood isn't food for thought, exactly:
    thought, when it comes,
    often comes to naught
and at the drop of a yarmulke or hat.
Imagine that! What luck to be in a sulk.

Jonas Salk, was he a Jew, too? Did he go to
    Hebrew school to dream, like a fool,
    of his vaccine in sugar-cube:
not so bracing sweet nor worthy of a stir
like, you should pardon the great American expression,
    Sure! How coy I'm not with this fifties-
    through-sixties boomer gruel:
Don't be cruel, I kid you not, twelve full ounces,
that's a lot in the sweet by-and-by, farther along,
    If loving you is wrong,
    I don't wanna be right, Dad.

SCRABBLE. MONOPOLY. Impervious,
implacable, impossible to appease, no pleasing
      some people, *sheesh! Puhleeze!*
Domestic bliss is, after all, hit or miss, like
dubiosity, ignorance, or even a disease
to be expunged by vaccination, not vacillation: action.
      Impatience married to a kitchen sponge.
      The middle son held, at length, his tongue.
What salvation? How did I spell relief? From filthy looks
I fled to my books—no paradise lost, there—books
and silent seething passages of time, thought, and labor.
      My ardor was for phantasm: grisly history
      and tawny novel of Civil Wars, World's
Great Classics, anything voluptuous, anything to quiet
fuss, any story but the one about us, e.g.,
      the one about my Jewish bootlegger grandfather
      sent to a Federal prison with bread and water,
my infant, speechless dad visiting him by train, in the South,
the bitterness in his mouth till his own death, never to unravel
      the Hydra's sticky arms of harsh speech
      and hideous hum in his anger-maze, and tedium.
Pent like a serpent, unrepentant, like unraveling Borealis in starlight.

No, you can't henpeck yourself.
You can't feel ice thin. Even so,
      when you say, "I feel like killing myself,"
      that syllogism leads
not to a philosophy of form, but to endless
analysis of act, vicious cycles of your own
rights and necessity. Oh, how cause-and-effect
      leaves one in the lurch! Essentially,
anger is unbecoming. Its conclusion appears

as an infinitely distant point I can approach
        only asymptotically, which is avowedly
        not to overlook the pure sound of emotion.
Just so, a cry becomes a word, the word becomes
a sentence, objectively, a *signum prefixum*.

Fix him? Did you just call me a Frankenstein?
Boo-fricking-hoo! At least I didn't have the gall
        to become a major poet,
        all tears and liquid *pro quo*. Or liquor
myself up with experience of the Thou, asking
what this "Thou" is saying to "us," and so on,
        or the "necessary separation of ourselves
        from ourselves . . ." Because forgetting
is so close to remembering*—mneme, anamnesis—
I'm sorry to be so tactless, but tact is tacit.
        I know it sounds like I'm taking the high
        road of *eruditio*, but I assure ya
I espouse the probable, not the true, the verisimilar.
Let's break the ice and lose these anticipations
and predilections: all art begins with the particular,

has lots of heart, and ends in sadness, fuckit—
if punctuation is biographical (God help our squandermania),
then I'm stuck like Delmore's glass-eyed duck in the bucket.

* This requires the power of abstraction, and a sense of humor. Um, *Bildung*.

Honi soit...
Royal Order of the Garter

"Honi soit quit mal y pense," my father
Mistranslated, and misconstrued, as "Evil
To him who evil does," missing the point. Oh,
I thought about, yet never did evil to my father
Though he cursed and bruised me and saw no evil
In doing so. If he ever laid a hand on a garter,
Would its likely owner, my mother, have wished to appoint
Such bent violence in offering to her own offspring?
Yes, she would, anointing it without even thinking.
So I took his violence unbeaten, as an honor, unblinking.
If my father only knew what was brewing! Each blow
Had rectitude, blessing, intimacy, and a ring
Of the implicative. Yet I did not suppose I was suffering,
Or that he was wicked. Now, a badge of honor, I still don't.

Bookish Men

My mother was apparently quoting Burke
When she would say, *The age of chivalry is gone*—
Not aptly, though, given her conquering empire
Of barbed irrationality: her marriage
Of inconvenience to Dad, the oafish sons he'd sire,
Not men-at-arms, but men-at-home. . . . berserk
Merciless chivvying, charmless chipping down to bone
In the cheerless shire of shared sham and rage.
The chirography on my birthday cards no relief,
Familiar rites for forty years. Fruitless now to wonder.
A gentleman always carries a handkerchief,
A gentleman never asks a woman her age,
Were not Burke; she sent us into lifelong solitude
Through repetition . . . bookish men, old for our years, rude.

A Drop in the Bucket

My mother, not quoting Coleridge: *Water, water*
everywhere, not a single drop to drink.
"Nor" was not her style, nor was her addition
of "single" or dropping of "and" singular.
She added many a word to what my father
failed to say, or said. This was the rule in her
extempore kingdom of sentences and kitchen sink.
She was well-spoken . . . unlike my father, dryly brilliant
scientist who seldom said more than he meant—
nothing token, quotable, or extravagant.
Words, to Dad, were data, nothing to be spoken;
to Mom, syllables strung together, each a token.
My mother wanted to be remembered and quoted;
her magisterium was full-bore, lachrymose, full-throated.

Ontogeny

Recapitulates phylogeny, my mother misquoted.
An admirable *extempore Orator pro Harangue*,
Her world was "hideous undelightful convulsed constricted,"*
but in her Penelope's work (*semper* fidelities), weaving
and unweaving maternity, she bent our lumpen tongues
which like boxwood were not easily shaped by the lathe.
There was good and plenty for us to feed on and loathe:
Father's raising crows to peck our eyes out.
Uncle's dying prematurely from a clot.
Our playing at risk of punishment on the spot.
In the end there was too much preoccupation with grieving,
But never mind: among one-eyed fathers mom is blind.
We each began as fingerlings resembling tadpoles, near-fish.
This was our first history. Phylogeny, after all, is selfish.

---

* Arnold on Brontë

Murder

I.

Her first word was "murder."
Possessed by a dream for days
at a tender age,
wedding bells rang:
she had it again.
A cloud compacified with thunder,
she haunted her lover into matrimony.
No one caught the bouquet.
There were no bridesmaids.
Her father reached for his knife,
a close shave.
Her white dress spoiled
where the groom pricked her
with the corsage pin: ritual
absorbed, the bloodstain patulous.

It was murderous, but it held,
at first, no children present
or past. Then, moving through the fringes
of their neighborhood, where tiny shadows
in the womb played furtively,
they embraced childlessness—
but not for long.

II.

Hers was a jiggle-the-handle town,
superstringed with coves, groves, and culs-de-sac,
in which nobody dared pee on the roses,
and nice days crossed
everyone's mind like murder.

Saturation. Incubation. Illumination.
What were the original dimensions of their space together?
What the odds of filling or fulfilling it?
Reddening tomatoes on a sill,
the late chill in September,
or horizons toward which clouds reach
with dark or light nimbus.
The peace of sunset following
the afternoon's long whirlwind:
even in murderous places, birds still sing.
Then, the commuter train's homebound
whistle-and-braking,
a single cat moaning . . .

"Everything I have," each home seems to say,
"I worked for.
This is all I have to show for it."

Why wasn't God's eldest a plumber, not a carpenter?
Time, unlike wood, and like water, runs
past our grasp of it—
wood suffers its deep anguish,
burns, at worst.
But water is never reducible to tears.
In that neighborhood, the hammering,
watering, sowing and mowing
never ends, just as it never began.
Therefore, when an owl calls
or a dog vocalizes,
when a car engine whinges
or a front door slams,
a child's singular cry is lost:
a coldly cellular anxiety

makes itself at home
in a tree house,
languishes murder,
the first word spoken.

III.

Into a marriage of inconvenience
she was born, and into another she entered.
Unknown to her parents or husband,
she would learn to speak "of the best-laid
plans of mice and me . . ."
A bone in the tarpits of shame,
honoring which her grandparents always put out
milk for their dead,
since body and soul agree
to yearn equally
for fidelity even when parted.
Insinuation, panache, and loss:
she was born into the symbolism of her subjection,
the daughter who doubled meaning,
disenchanted, disobliged: *murdered.*

The Comedy of Clocks

The multilingual wind licks
the Babel on the plain where I have the stink
and linger of bad faith and errata

upon me. Cogging and cringing
though work, moth of my days,
my new family fleers on me.

Where is the interim
of my time? Is the scratting
crow bad luck or good?

Mad structures, useless buildings—
I sit on the stone of turpitude
with my ass bared, eviscerating

myself like a spider in study.
Which is why my ex-
wife halved us: I

couldn't carve at table,
and like any swasher I was a scholar,
a clown, a mere donkey

in wartime, worth questionable
even as I questioned:
Perfection—do I look it up under

life or *work*? My tortoise-
shell glasses are so far from the lyre
Mercury fashioned for Apollo

when even the gods were
still stepchildren, lost
in the sandbox, in earth.

She and I grew up together,
and apart together.
We swam in the same place,

if not in the same numerical water.
Why did she cross the river
of knowledge without me?

The Dead Language

I stopped taking care of myself on the theory
well there was no theory just the tedium
of self-effect something inward grew
and grew I refuse to call it a polyp
on the grounds that this sounds cultivated
and terminiological, God, anything but *that!*
the Romans said poets have the right
and power to kill themselves if they want,
that to save someone can be just as wrong
as to murder him, though they said it
in the dead language, Latin, whose
satisfactions are not altogether lost
yes a few virtues are what make us human
the rest is death, and like a poet
a man should stick to his very last
so please give me what I have or even less
then let me live for what's left of my life

On Original Intent

If I look lost
in thought, maybe nobody
will take my picture,
and I won't have to go
into the all-in-one
printer/scanner/copier/fax
for a change
to have my image spread
over the internet like a dead
man or wanted criminal.
It's not like the scratchy old
days of black and white
waves of mass migrations
to America:
sudden greenhorns cantered
with tilting pushcarts, or balanced
bales of fresh matzoh on their heads,
as they trekked across the bold
cobbles of their world-
of-our-fathers Lower East Side.

I saw the documentary,
read the book, bought the T-
shirt and soundtrack, all
of which neglected
to answer the main question:
Why do we say
take a picture, anyway?
So that someday
we can bequeath them to
our glib survivors, who'll stare
down and guzzle memory

like oil?
So they can take
a minute of their by-then-
precious time to wonder
what in hell we were
doing here back in wartime when
people like me were still alive?

Agitated, I offer to give my
wife a hand, which is probably
going to bug her,
and really, what is
to be done in time
of pandemic, anyway:
Laundry? Halloween decos?
The skulls and pumpkins
of October ogle our love-smeared
preschoolers who are damned
if they do, damned if they
don't in their pre-
packaged celluloid capes, faces gory-
painted like apples in all their crisp glory.
Lined up two-by-two on
a field trip to the fire
station, our tiny descendants absorb
such survivalist tips as how
to rescue an orange kitty from a tree
or what meaning lies in the story
of Sparky in a safety-tip coloring book.

Well, it's either all that memorable
stuff or laughing in photogenic
astonishment as somebody's

visiting workingdaddy does a scarf-
dance, plays "Puff
the Magic Dragon" on his trusty Gibson,
talks about seeing the Red Sox with grandpa,
or fills in his little-lamb son
and daughter about the framers of that old
chestnut, *The Constitution of the United
States of America.*

Notes:

"If the dam trot, the foal will not amble," "glue or lime with which the wings of the mind once taken cannot fly away," "mad structures," "stone of turpitude," "smack of this disease," and parts of the poem, "Sweet Water, Best Bread" are from Robert Burton, *The Anatomy of Melancholy*.

Information about scorpions waltzing and sounds caterpillars make to get ants to care for them is from a book review by Tim Flannery, "When a Scorpion Meets a Scorpion," *The New York Review of Books*, March 23, 2006.

"single concealed point" is from a book review by Jeremy Adler, "Kabbala Then and Now," *Times Literary Supplement*, February 22, 2006.

"While the horse starves, the grass grows," paraphrased in this book, is an Italian proverb.

"Everything has two handles, one by which it may be borne; another by which it cannot," paraphrased in this book, is from Epictetus.

"like crow, like egg" is a Latin proverb.

"they do not grant halves in heaven" is from the Talmud, T. B. Yoma, 69b.

"incline but do not require" is from "Knowledge and Coherence," by Paul Thagard, Chris Eliasmith, Paul Rusnock, and Cameron Shelley, online at: http://cogsci.uwaterloo.ca/Articles/Pages/epistemic.html

"Justice is Conflict" is the title of a book by Stuart Hampshire.

"the freshening of Atlantic waters" is from a book review by Bill McKibben, "Crossing the Red Line," *The New York Review of Books*, June 10, 2004.

"not that we did evolve from birds; we were only reptiles together" and "emotion devoid of earth" are from *Music and Speech* by Katharine M. Wilson.

"staggered tandem over time" is from a book review by Frederick C. Crews, "Saving Us from Darwin," *The New York Review of Books*, October 4, 2001.

"want of fruitfulness" is from Bacon's essay, "Of Building."

"Rotten Child Theorem" is actually Gary Becker's Rotten Kid Theorem; see "A Theory of Social Interactions," *Journal of Political Economy*, 82, 1063–1093.

"infinitely distant point I can approach only asymptotically" is rephrased from Ernst Cassirer.

"the separation of ourselves from ourselves" is from Paul Tillich, *The Shaking of the Foundations*.

"Art begins with the particular" is attributed to Flannery O'Connor.

"The trail of the human serpent is thus over everything," paraphrased in this book, is from William James, "What Pragmatism Means," Lecture 2 in *Pragmatism*.

Lightning Source UK Ltd.
Milton Keynes UK
UKHW01f1325210618
324570UK00001B/57/P